Contact Us!

Dr. Nicki Newton

Email: gigglenook@gmail.com

Website: www.drnicki123.com

Blog: guidedmath.wordpress.com

Also by Dr. Nicki Newton

PROBLEM SOLVING™

WITH MATH MODELS

FIFTH GRADE

DR. NICKI NEWTON

GigglePublications
hook
Math with a Smile

Gigglenook Publication
P.O. Box 110134
Trumbull CT 06611
Email: gigglenook@gmail.com
Website: www.drnicki123.com

Produced by GiggleNook Publications
Thank you to the entire Production staff

Chief Operating Officer: Dr. Nicki Newton
Publisher: Gigglenook Publication
Cover Design: This Way Up Productions
Text Design and Composition: Bonnie Harrison-Jones

Printed in the United States of America
ISBN-13: 978-1493522330
ISBN-10: 1493522337
Volume 1: December 2012

Dedicated to Mom and Pops, Always

TABLE OF CONTENTS

FOREWORD

Story problems can be great! Story problems are the stuff life is made of. If we can make connections for children between their daily lives and the problems we pose and solve in school, we will have much more success. We need to provide scaffolds into the process.

The New Math Common Core (CCSS, 2010) places a big emphasis on problem solving. The first mathematical practice mentioned states that students should "Make sense of problems and persevere in solving them." It goes on to describe this by stating that mathematically proficient students should be able to explain a problem and find ways to enter into it. According to the New Math Common Core students should be able to solve problems with objects, drawings and equations. In this book, students will practice word problems aligned to the standards by using the CCSS designated math models.

The Math Common Core, actually adopted the framework for story problems, created by Carpenter, Fennema, Franke, Levi & Empson, 1999; Peterson, Fennema & Carpenter (1989). The research says that the more teachers understand these types of problems and teach them to their students, the better students understand the problems and are able to solve them. Furthermore, the research makes the case that the KEY WORD METHOD should be avoided! Students should learn to understand the problem types and what they are actually discussing rather than "key word" tricks. The thing about key words is that they only work with really simplistic problems and so as students do more sophisticated work with word problems, the key words do not serve them well. They may actually lead them in the wrong direction, often encouraging the wrong operation. For example, given this problem: *John has 2 apples. Kate has 3 more than he does. How many do they have altogether?* Many students just add 2 and 3 instead of unpacking the problem. Another example, given this problem: *Sue has 10 marbles. She has 2 times as many marbles as Lucy. How many marbles does Lucy have?*

Often times, students just multiply because they see the word times, instead of really reading and understanding the problem.

This book is about giving students a repertoire of tools, models and strategies to help them think about, understand and solve word problems. We want to scaffold reasoning opportunities from the concrete (using objects) to the pictorial (pictures and drawings) and, finally, to the abstract (writing equations).

DR. NICKI NEWTON

ACKNOWLEDGEMENTS

I would like to thank many people for their support, expertise, guidance, and encouragement during this project. First of all, I would like to thank God, without Him this would not be possible. Second, I would like to thank my mom, pa, big mom, and granddaddy. Third, I would like to thank my family for all their love and support, especially my Tia that calls me every day and asks, "What have you accomplished today?" And finally, I would like to thank all of my friends who support me all the time. This book series would not have been possible without the continual support of the Gigglenook Production Team. Thank you all!

INTRODUCTION TO THE TYPES OF PROBLEMS

Grade Specific Problem Solving Expectations

The CCSS is very specific about what students should be able to do in terms of solving word problems by grade level. There are 4 general categories for addition and subtraction problems. In kindergarten students are exposed to 4 problem types - 1 addition, 1 subtraction, and 2 part/part whole problems. They are expected to work with these types of problems through 10. But, in first grade, there is a big leap. The standards say that the children will be able to work with the above-mentioned four problems, in addition to addition and subtraction change unknown problems, the other part/ part whole problem as well as comparison problems with unknowns in all positions and with a symbol for the unknown to represent the problem through 20. Students should also be able to solve word problems with three numbers adding up to 20. By second grade, they have to be able to solve all problem types, including the harder comparison problems through 100. In 3rd through 5th grade the students should be able to solve all of the problem types using larger whole numbers, fractions and decimals.

Adding to Problems

"Adding to" problems are all about adding. There are three types. The first type is *Adding to* problems where the result is unknown. For example, *Jenny had 5 marbles. John gave her 3 more. How many marbles does Jenny have now?* In this problem the result is unknown. Teachers tend to tell these types of problems. They are basic and straightforward. The teacher should start with concrete items, then proceed to drawing out the story, then to diagramming the story, and finally to using equations to represent the story. This is the easiest type of story problem to solve.

The second kind of *Adding to* problem is the "Change Unknown" problem. For example, *Jenny had 5 marbles. John gave her some more. Now she has 8 marbles. How many marbles did John give her?* In this type of problem, the students are looking for the change. They know the start and they know the end but they don't know the *change*. So, students have to put down the start and then count up to find how many. Students could also start with 8 marbles and take away the original 5 to see how many more were added to make 8.

The third type of *Adding to* Problem is a "Start Unknown" problem. For example, *Jenny had some marbles. John gave her 3 more. Now she has 8 marbles. How many marbles did Jenny have in the beginning?* In this type of problem, the students are looking for the start. This is the hardest type of *adding to* problem to solve. This takes a great deal of modeling.

Taking From Problems

Taking From problems are all about subtracting. There are three types. The first type is *taking from* problems where the result is unknown. For example, *Jenny had 5 marbles. She gave John 3. How many marbles does Jenny have left?* In this problem, the result is unknown. Teachers tend to tell these types of problems. They are basic and straightforward. The teacher should start with concrete items, then proceed to drawing out the story, then to diagramming the story, and finally to writing equations to represent the story.

The second kind of *Taking From* problem is the "Change Unknown" problem. For example, *Jenny had 10 marbles. She gave John some. Now she has 8 marbles left. How many marbles did she give to John?* In this type of problem, the students are looking for the change. They know the start and they know the end but they don't know the *change*. So, students have to put down the start and then count up to find how many. Students could also start with 10 marbles and take away some until they have 8 left. They would count to see how many they had to take away to remain with 8.

The third type of *Taking From* problem is a "Start Unknown" problem. For example, *Jenny had some marbles. She gave John 3. Now she has 7 marbles left. How many marbles did Jenny have to start with?* In this type of problem, the students are looking for the start. This is the hardest type of *taking from* problem to solve. This takes a great deal of modeling. You can use ten frames to show this. One strategy is to have the students put down the seven she has left and count up three to see how many that makes.

Part/Part Whole Problems

A *Part/Part Whole* problem is a problem that discusses the two parts and the whole. There are three types of *Part/Part Whole* Problems. The first is a problem where the *whole* is unknown. For example, *Susie has some marbles. Five are red and five are blue. How many marbles does she have altogether?* We know both parts and the task is to figure out the whole.

The second kind of problem is a problem where one of the *parts* is unknown. For example, *Susie has 10 marbles. Seven are red. The rest are blue. How many are blue?* In this type of problem, we are given the whole and one of the parts. The task is to figure out the other part.

The third type of problem is a *Both Addends Unknown* problem. In this type of problem both addends are not known, only the total is given. For example, *There are 4 frogs on the log. Some are blue and some are green. There are some of each color. How many of each color could there be?* The task is to figure out all the possible combinations.

Comparing Stories

Comparing Stories are the most difficult types of stories to tell. There are three types of comparison stories. The first type of comparison story is where two different things are being compared. For example, *Susie has ten lollipops and Kayla has eight. How many more lollipops does Susie have than Kayla?*

The second type of comparison story is where the bigger part is unknown. In this type of story, we are looking for the bigger amount. For example, *Susie had 4 candies. Maya had 3 more than her. How many candies did Maya have?* Here, we know what Susie had, and then in comparison, Maya had 3 more. The task is to find the bigger part.

The third type of comparison story is to find the smaller part. This is the hardest type of story to tell. For example, *Jaya has 7 candies. She has 3 more than Marcos. How many does Marcos have?* In this type of story we know what Jaya has and we know that she has 3 more than Marcos. We are looking for the smaller amount. We only know about what Marcos has in comparison to what Jaya has. The task is to use the information given to solve for the smaller part.

Introduction to the 5th Grade Standards and the Models for Thinking

The CCSSM (2010) requires that students model their thinking in a variety of ways. In 5th grade students are expected to have mastered all the things they have learned in k-4. Throughout this book, problems are given and students are required to model them in the way that the standards describe in terms of addition and subtraction. In 5th grade students should be able to:

Solve multistep word problems posed with whole numbers and having whole-number answers using the four operations, including problems in which remainders must be interpreted. **Represent these problems using equations with a letter standing for the unknown quantity**. Assess the reasonableness of answers using mental computation and estimation strategies including rounding. (*Students have been working on multi-step word problems sense 2nd grade.*)

Solve word problems involving addition and subtraction of fractions referring to the same whole, including cases of unlike denominators e.g. by using visual fraction models or equations to represent the problem. (*Students have been working on fraction problems sense 3rd grade. This standard is 5NF2.*)

Students should be able to discuss and illustrate their thinking about comparing decimals to thousandths as well as adding, subtracting, multiplying and dividing them, using concrete models, or drawing and strategies based on place value, properties of operations, and/or the relationship between addition and subtraction; relate the strategy to a written method and explain the reasoning used. (*Students have been working with decimals sense 4th grade but the deep work is started in 5th. This standard is 5NF7.*)

Convert among different-sized standard measurement units within a given measurement system and use the conversions in solving multi-step, real world problems. *(Students have been working on measurement word problems since 2ⁿᵈ grade. This standard is 5MD1.)*

Make a line plot to display a data set of measurements in fractions of a unit (1/2, 1/4, 1/8). Use operations on fractions for this grade to solve problems involving information presented in line plots. *(Students have been working with line plots since 2ⁿᵈ grade. This standard is 5MD2.)*

Relate volume to the operations of multiplication and addition and solve real world and mathematical problems involving volume. *(Liquid volume is introduced in 3ʳᵈ grade however the majority of volume work is introduced in 5ᵗʰ grade. This standard is 5MD5.)*

USE BAR/TAPE DIAGRAM

In the CCSSM students are required to know how to use a tape diagram to model their thinking. *Bar diagrams help students to "unpack" the structure of a problem and lay the foundation for its solution" (Diezmann and English, 2001, p. 77 cited in Charles, Monograph 24324). Nickerson (1994) found that the ability to use diagrams is integral to mathematics thinking and learning (cited in Charles).*

In the charts below, I have provided a detailed explanation for each of the CCSS 1-step word problem types for addition and subtraction. The word problem type is designated with a sample problem. Then there is a bar diagram to show the relationships between the quantities. Then there is an explanation of the problem type and the various strategies that can be used to solve the problem. There is also the algebraic equation showing the different operations that can be used to solve the problem. As Charles (Monograph 24324) points out, *"It is important to recognize that a relationship in some word problems can be translated into more than one appropriate number sentence."*

Problem Types	Result Unknown	Change Unknown	Start Unknown
Join/Adding to	Marco had 5 marbles. His brother gave him 5 more. How many does he have now?	Marco had 5 marbles. His brother gave him some more. Now he has 10. How many did his brother give him?	Marco had some marbles. His brother gave him 5 more. Now he has 10. How many did he have in the beginning
Bar Diagram Modeling Problem	? ⟵⟶ [5 | 5]	10 ⟵⟶ [5 | ?]	10 ⟵⟶ [? | 5]
What are we looking for? Where is X?	Both addends are known. We are looking for the total amount. The result is the unknown. In other words, we know what we started with and we know the change, we are looking for the end.	The first addend is known. The result is also known. We are looking for the change. The change is unknown. In other words, we know what happened at the start and we know what happened at the end. We are looking for the change. We need to find out what happened in the middle.	The second addend is known. The result is known. We are looking for the start. The start is unknown. In other words, we know the change and we know the end but we don't know what happened at the beginning.
Algebraic Sentence	5 + 5 = ?	5 + ?= 10 10-5=?	x + 5 = 10
Strategies to Solve	Add/ Know number Bonds/Know derived Facts/ Count Up	Count Up/Know Bonds/	Count up/Subtract
Answer	5 + 5 = 10 He had ten marbles.	5 + 5 = 10 10 - 5 = 5 He brother gave him five marbles.	5 + 5 = 10 10 - 5 = 5 He had five marbles.

Problem Types	Result Unknown	Change Unknown	Start Unknown
Separate/ Taking From	Marco had 10 marbles. He gave his brother 4. How many does he have left?	Marco had 10 marbles. He gave some away. Now he has 5 left. How many did he give away?	Marco had some marbles. He gave 2 away and now he has 5 left. How many did he have to start with?
Bar Diagram Modeling Problem	10 ⟷ / 4 | ?	10 ⟷ / ? | 5	? ⟷ / 2 | 5
What are we looking for? Where is X?	In this story we know the beginning and what happened in the middle. The mystery is what happened at the end. The result is unknown.	In this story we know the beginning and the end. The mystery is what happened in the middle. The change is unknown.	In this story we know what happened in the middle and what happened at the end. The mystery is how did it start. The start is unknown.
Algebraic Sentence	$10 - 4 = ?$	$10 - ? = 5$ $5 + x = 10$	$? - 2 = 5$ $2 + 5 = ?$
Strategies to Solve	Subtract/ /Use number Bonds Facts/ Know derived Facts (Doubles -1, Doubles -2)	Subtract until you have the result left/ Count Up/Use number Bonds/Use derived facts	Count up/Subtract
Answer	$10-4 = 6$ He had 6 marbles left.	$10-5=5$ $5 + 5 = 10$ He gave away 5 marbles.	$7-2 = 5$ $2+5 = 7$ He had 7 marbles in the beginning.

Problem Solving with Math Models© 2012

Problem Types	Quantity Unknown	Part Unknown	Both Addends Unknown
Part/Part Whole/Putting together/Taking Apart	Marco has 5 red marbles and 5 blue ones. How many marbles does Marco have? 5 + 5 = x	Marco has 10 marbles. Five are red and the rest are blue. How many are blue? 10 -5 = or 5 + x = 10	Marco has 10 marbles. Some are red and some are blue. How many could be red and how many could be blue?
Bar Diagram Modeling Problem	? 5 5	10 5 ?	10 ? ?
What are we looking for? Where is X?	In this type of story we are talking about a group, set or collection of something. Here we know both parts and we are looking for the total.	In this type of story we are talking about a group, set or collection of something. Here we know the total and one of the parts. We are looking for the amount of the other part.	In this type of story we are talking about a group set or collection of something. Here we know the total but we are to think about all the possible ways to make the group, set or collection.
Algebraic Sentence	5 + 5 = ?	5 + ? = 10 10-5=?	x + y = 10
Strategies to Solve	Add/ Know number Bonds/Know derived Facts/ Count Up	Count Up/Know Bonds/	Count up/Subtract
Answer	5+5=10 He had ten marbles.	5+5=10 10-5 =? Five were blue	1+9 4+6 9+1 6+4 2+8 5+5 8 + 2 3+7 10+0 0 +10 7+3 These are the possibilities

Problem Types	Difference Unknown	Bigger Part Unknown	Smaller Part Unknown
Compare	Marco has 5 marbles. His brother has 7. How many more marbles does his brother have than he does?	Marco has 5 marbles. His brother has 2 more than he does. How many marbles does his brother have?	Tom has 5 rocks. Marco has 2 less than Tom. How many rocks does Marco have?
Bar Diagram Modeling Problem	5 ? 7	5 / 5 2 / ?	5 / ?
What are we looking for? Where is X?	In this type of story we are comparing two amounts. We are looking for the difference between the two numbers.	In this type of story we are comparing two amounts. We are looking for the bigger part which is unknown.	In this type of story we are comparing two amounts. We are looking for the smaller part which is unknown.
Algebraic Sentence	7-5 =?	5 + ? = 7	5-2=?
Strategies to Solve	Count up/ Count back	Count up	Subtract
Answer	His brother had 2 more marbles than he did.	His brother had 7 marbles.	Marco had 3 marbles.

Teacher Tips:

❋ When you introduce the problem, be sure to tell the students what type of problem it is.

❋ Remember that you can take the same problem and rework it in different ways throughout the week.

❋ Work on a problem type until the students are proficient at recognizing and solving that problem type. Also give them opportunities to write and tell that specific problem type.

❋ Be sure to contextualize the problems in the students' everyday lives. Using the problems in the book as models, substitute the students' names and their everyday things.

❋ Be sure to provide tons of guided practice. Solve problems together as a class, with partners and in groups. Individual practice should come after the students have had plenty of opportunities to work together and comprehend and understand what they are doing.

❋ Emphasize that there is no one correct way to solve a problem but that there is usually only one correct answer.

❋ *Encourage students to always show their work

CHAPTER 1
ADD TO RESULT UNKNOWN PROBLEMS

These types of problems are the easiest types of addition problems. In these problems students are looking for what happened at the end of the story. We know what we started with and what we added to that part. We are trying to find out how many we have altogether now.

PROBLEM	John had 10 marbles. Henry gave him 7 more. How many does he have now?
MODEL	
EQUATION	10 + 7 = ? 10 + 7 = 17

ADD TO RESULT UNKNOWN

1. Jonathan drank 2 quarts of chocolate milk in the morning. Later that day he drank another 2 pints. How many pints did he drink altogether?

Way#1: Use a drawing to model your thinking

Way#2: Solve with numbers

Explain your thinking:

ADD TO RESULT UNKNOWN

2. Sue had $259.22 saved. Her grandmother gave her $58.88 for her birthday. Her sister gave her $44.77. How much does she have now?

Solve with numbers

Explain your thinking:

ADD TO RESULT UNKNOWN

3.   Tom the baker used 1/2 cup of flour in his cake. Then, he added 3/4 a cup of flour. How much flour did he use altogether?

Model with a Tape Diagram

Explain your thinking:

ADD TO RESULT UNKNOWN

4. Lisa made fruit punch for her party. First she added 589 ml of orange juice. Next, she added 798 ml of apple juice. Finally, she added 834 ml of pineapple juice. How many liters of fruit punch did she make?

Way#1: Model with a drawing (use beakers)

Way#2: Represent your thinking with an equation

Explain your thinking:

ADD TO RESULT UNKNOWN

5. On the internet, Song A had 245,777 views in the morning and 43,876 more views in the evening. What was the total amount of views for Song A?

Way#1: Solve with an equation

Way#2: Check in a different way

Explain your thinking:

ADD TO RESULT UNKNOWN

6. The jeweler cut several inches of gold rope. Here are ~~their~~ there lengths: 1/4, 1/4, 1/4, 1/4, 2/4, 2/4, 3/4 ,3/4, 3/4 and 4/4.

Way#1: Make a line plot for the data

Way#2: What was the total amount of rope that the jeweler cut?

Explain your thinking:

ADD TO RESULT UNKNOWN

7. Luke's family went on vacation. They drove 145.6 miles and then stopped for lunch. After lunch they drove 179.88 miles. What was the total amount of miles that they drove?

Way#1: Model with a bar diagram

Way#2: Write an equation

Explain Your Thinking:

ADD TO RESULT UNKNOWN

8. Trish had 500 cm of string. She bought 300 more cm. She needed 7 meters. Will she have enough? How much will she have in meters?

Create a table to show your thinking

Centimeters	Meters
	1

Explain your answer

CHAPTER 1 QUIZ: ADD TO RESULT UNKNOWN

Solve with a model:

1. Jen ran 2.34 miles. Then she ran another 3.7 miles. How far did she run?

2. Clay made some fruit punch. He put in 1.5 liters of pineapple juice. He put in 457 ml of apple juice. He put in 2.7 liters of coconut juice. How many ml of juice did he use?

3. Grandma Betsy was making a supersize pie. She added 3/4 cup of sugar into the pie. Then she added 2/8 of a cup more. She decided she needed a bit more so she added 1/8 cup more. How much sugar did she use altogether?

4. Raul bought 4 yards of wood. Then he went back to the store and bought 4.5 more feet of wood. How many yards of wood did he buy altogether?

CHAPTER 2
ADD TO CHANGE UNKNOWN PROBLEMS

In these problems students are looking for what happened in the middle of the story. In this type of story we know what happened at the beginning but then some change happened and now we have more than we started with at the end. We are trying to find out how many things were added in the middle of the story.

PROBLEM	John had 5 marbles. His mother gave him some more. Now he has 12. How many did his mother give him?
MODEL	
EQUATION	5 + ? = 12 5 + 7 = 12

ADD TO CHANGE UNKNOWN

1. The candy store had 459 grams of chocolate fudge. They got a new shipment and now have 2 kilograms of chocolate fudge. How much fudge did they get in the shipment?

Way#1: Solve with a number line

Way#2: Solve with an equation, use a letter for the unknown

Explain your thinking:

ADD TO CHANGE UNKNOWN

2. Raul went to the baseball field at 5:28. He was there for a while and then he went home. He went home at 6:07. How long was he gone?

Solve with a number line diagram

Explain your thinking:

ADD TO CHANGE UNKNOWN

3. Grandma Betsy made a cake. She put in 3/4 cup of sugar. She tasted the batter and decided to add more. In total, she put in 1 and 1/2 cups of sugar. How much sugar did she add?

Way#1: Solve with a number line

Way#2: Solve with an illustration

Explain your thinking:

ADD TO CHANGE UNKNOWN

4.   Donna made fruit punch for the party. She added 687 ml of cherry juice and then some apple juice. Altogether, she had 1.5 liters of juice. How much apple juice did she add?

Way#1: Draw a picture of a beaker to solve

Way#2: Solve with an equation, use a letter for the unknown

Explain your thinking:

ADD TO CHANGE UNKNOWN

5. Lisa had saved $53.19. She got some more money for her birthday. Now she has $70.00. How much money did she get for her birthday?

Way#1: Solve with an equation, use a letter for the unknown

Way#2: Solve another way

Explain your thinking:

Problem Solving with Math Models© 2012

ADD TO CHANGE UNKNOWN

6. Kenny and his 2 friends went into the store. They wanted to buy some candy that cost $2.00. Kenny pulled ¾ of a dollar out of his pocket. John added ½ of a dollar. How much money did Tim have to add to get to $2.00?

Way#1: Solve with an open number line

Way#2: Solve with an equation, use a letter for the unknown

Explain your thinking:

ADD TO CHANGE UNKNOWN

7. John made 5000 ml of punch. Then he made some more. Now he has 8.1 liters of punch. How much more did he make?

Way#1: Solve with drawing

Way#2: Solve with an equation, use a letter for the unknown

Explain your thinking:

ADD TO CHANGE UNKNOWN

8. Baker John used 5 1/2 pounds of flour. Then, he used some more. He used a total of 7 3/4 pounds of flour. How much flour did he add?

Way#1: Model with a tape diagram

Way#2: Solve with an equation, use a letter for the unknown

Explain your thinking:

CHAPTER 2 QUIZ: ADD TO CHANGE UNKNOWN PROBLEMS

Solve with a model:

1. Sue left her house at 12:21. She went to the mall and then to her friend's house. She got home at 5:03. How long was she gone?

2. Luke made a soup. He put in 1.5 liters of water. After he tasted it, he added more ml of water. When he finished, he had used 3000 ml of water. How many liters of water did he add?

Problem Solving with Math Models© 2012

3. Troy ran 9/10 of a mile in the morning. In the afternoon he ran some more. In total, he ran 2.5 miles. How far did he run in the afternoon?

4. Maria had $37.43. She got some more money for her birthday. Now she has $55.22. How much did she get for her birthday?

In these problems students are looking for what happened in the beginning of the story. In this type of story we know what happened in the middle and we know how many we ended up with but we are looking for how the story started.

PROBLEM	John had some marbles. Henry gave him 7 more. Now he has 14. How many did he have in the beginning?
MODEL	
EQUATION	$? + 7 = 14$ $7 + 7 = 14$

ADD TO START UNKNOWN

1. Song A had several downloads from the Internet in the morning. In the afternoon, Song A got 47,894 more downloads. Now it has 55,987 downloads all total. How many downloads did it have in the morning?

Way#1: Solve with numbers

Way#2: Check in a different way

Explain your thinking:

ADD TO START UNKNOWN

2. Mr. Chi went to the mall for 5 hours and 15 minutes. He then went to his friend's house for 2 and a half hours. He came back to his house at 7:15. What time did he leave her house originally?

Solve with a number line diagram

Explain your thinking:

Problem Solving with Math Models© 2012

ADD TO START UNKNOWN

3. Jake had some money. For his birthday, his brother and sister gave him some more. His brother gave him 10 quarters. His sister gave him 200 pennies. Now he has $20.00. How much did he have in the beginning?

Way#1: Solve with a drawing

Way#2: Solve with an equation, use a letter for the unknown

Explain your thinking:

ADD TO START UNKNOWN

4. The Johnsons drove some miles and then stopped to have lunch. After lunch, they drove 25.78 more miles. Altogether, they drove 100 miles. How many miles did they drive before lunch?

Model with an equation, use a letter for the unknown

Explain your thinking:

ADD TO START UNKNOWN

5. The school cook made some liters of fruit punch. He then made 1500 more ml. Altogether, he made 7 liters of fruit punch. How many liters of fruit punch did he have in the beginning?

Way#1: Model with a drawing

Way#2: Solve with an equation, use a letter for the unknown

Explain your thinking:

ADD TO START UNKNOWN

6. Chef Luke made a big pot of gumbo. He started with some shrimp. He added 1.5 kilograms of clams. He also added 987 g of mussels. Altogether he used 5 kilograms of seafood. How much shrimp did he use in the beginning?

Way#1: Model with a tape diagram

Way#2: Solve with an equation, use a letter for the unknown

Explain your thinking:

ADD TO START UNKNOWN

7. Raul plays lots of sports. He drank some water before he left home. At the basketball game, he drank 1 quart of water. He went for a run and drank 2 more pints. Then he went to the soccer game and drank 4 cups of water. Altogether he drank 1 gallon of water. How much liquid did he drink at the beginning of the day?

Solve

Explain your thinking:

ADD TO START UNKNOWN

8. Kate ran a bit in the morning. Then she ran 2 2/4 of a mile more. Altogether she ran 4 miles. How many miles did she run in the morning?

Way#1: Solve with a number line

Way#2: Solve with an equation, use a letter for the unknown

Explain your thinking:

Solve with a model:

1. Lisa had saved money to buy a dress. Her mother gave her $56.78 and her father gave her $39.77. Now she has $120. How much money did she have in the beginning?

2. Chung went to his grandmother's house for 2 1/2 hours. Then he went to the mall for 45 minutes. He came home at 5:25. What time did he leave his house?

3. Chef Jamal made a fancy soup. He put in some coconut juice and then he added 856 more ml of coconut juice. Altogether he used 1.5 liters of coconut juice. How much coconut juice did he use in the fancy soup in the beginning?

4. Song A had several hits in the morning. In the afternoon, it had 35,789 more hits. In total, there were 100,000 hits. How many hits were there in the morning?

UNIT 1 TEST:
ADDITION PROBLEMS

Solve with a model:

1. The jeweler cut some gold rope to make necklaces. Later he cut 88 cm more. Then he cut 49 cm more. Altogether he cut 2 meters of gold rope. How much did he cut at first?

2. Shakhira baked a cake. First, she put in 2/3 cup of sugar. Then she added 1/4 cup more. How much sugar did she use altogether?

3. Grandma Millie made a soup. She put in 1 quart of chicken stock. She tasted it and then added 2 more pints. She tasted it again and added 3 more cups. What is the total amount of chicken stock that she used? State your answer in cups, pints and quarts.

4. Grace had saved $45.45 for a dress that costs $80. Her mom gave her some money for her birthday. Now she only needs $10 more. How much did her mom give her?

Problem Solving with Math Models© 2012

CHAPTER 1
TAKE FROM RESULT UNKNOWN PROBLEMS

In these problems students are looking for what happened in the end of the story. In this type of story we know what happened at the beginning and also what change occurred. We are trying to find out how many things remained after some things were taken away.

PROBLEM	John had 10 apples. He gave 5 away. How many does he have left?
MODEL	
EQUATION	10 – ? = 5 10 – 5 = 5

TAKE FROM RESULT UNKNOWN

1. Kent had $352.11. He paid $55.88 for some shoes, $38.67 for some videos, and $207.55 for some clothes. How much money did he have left?

Way#1: Model with a tape diagram

Way#2: Model with an equation, use a letter for the unknown

Explain your thinking:

TAKE FROM RESULT UNKNOWN

2. Baker Maria loves to cook with coconut juice. She had 3 liters of juice. She used 598 ml in her cookies, 334 ml in her cakes and 789 ml in her pies. How many liters does she have left?

Way#1: Model with a tape diagram

Way#2: Solve with an equation, use a letter for the unknown

Explain your thinking:

TAKE FROM RESULT UNKNOWN

3. Don had 7.5 meters of wood. He decided to cut the wood into 100 centimeters to make a shelf. How many shelves could he make?

Way#1: Model with a table

Centimeters	Meters
100	**1**

Answer:

Explain your thinking:

Take From Result Unknown

4. Grandma Mary bought a gallon of milk. She used 2 pints in her super sized cake, 1 quart in her egg soup, 2 cups in her cookies and 2 cups in her pies. How many quarts does she have left? How many pints does she have left?

Way#1: Solve with a drawing

Way#2: Solve with an equation, use a letter for the unknown

Explain your thinking:

TAKE FROM RESULT UNKNOWN

5. Maria wanted to exercise for 2 and a half hours. She spent 45 minutes swimming, 47 minutes biking and 33 minutes on the treadmill. How long has she been exercising. How many more minutes does she need to exercise to complete a 2 1/2 hour exercise routine?

Solve with an open number line diagram

Explain your thinking

 Problem Solving with Math Models© 2012

TAKE FROM RESULT UNKNOWN

6. The bakery made a dozen cupcakes. The first customer bought 3/12 of them. The second customer bought 1/4 of them. The third customer bought 1/3 of them. How many of the cupcakes have they sold? How many are left?

Way#1: Model with a tape diagram

Way#2: Solve with an equation, use a letter for the unknown

Explain your thinking:

TAKE FROM RESULT UNKNOWN

7. Luke and his brother split a candy bar. Luke at 3/5 of the candy bar and his brother ate 2/10 of the candy bar. How much of the candy bar did they eat? How much is left?

Way#1: Solve with a drawing

Way#2: Solve with the formulas for perimeter and area. Show all your work.

Explain your thinking:

CHAPTER 1 QUIZ:
TAKE FROM RESULT UNKNOWN PROBLEMS

Solve with a model:

1. Joshua had $154.22. He spent $24.88 on games, $56.99 on shoes, and $49 on clothes. How much money did he have left?

2. The fruit stand had 3 kilos of apples. They sold 500 grams in the morning and 1000 more grams in the afternoon. How many kilos of apples did they have left?

3. Lucinda had 3 meters of string. She used 78 centimeters to make a necklace and 55 centimeters to make a bracelet. How many meters of string did she have left?

4. Grandma Joanie made some brownies. She cut them up into 12 pieces. John ate 1/4 of them. Sue ate 1/3 of them and Katy ate 2/12 of them. How many brownies were left?

CHAPTER 2
TAKE FROM CHANGE UNKNOWN PROBLEMS

In these problems students are looking for what happened in the middle of the story. In this type of story we know what happened at the beginning but then some change happened and now we have less than we started with by the end of the story. We are trying to find out how many things were taken away in the middle of the story.

PROBLEM	John had 15 marbles. He gave some to his cousin. Now he has 12 left. How many did he give to his cousin?
MODEL	
EQUATION	$15 - ? = 12$ $\qquad\qquad 15 - 3 = 12$

TAKE FROM CHANGE UNKNOWN

1. Grandma Annie used milk to cook. She had 2 quarts. She used 2 pints in her egg soup and the rest in her cakes. How much did she use in her cakes?

Way#1: Draw a picture

Way#2: Solve with an equation, use a letter for the unknown

Explain your thinking:

TAKE FROM CHANGE UNKNOWN

2. Don left his house at 12:20. He came back at 3:10. How long was he gone?

Solve with a number line

Explain your thinking:

TAKE FROM CHANGE UNKNOWN

3. Luke ate 1/5 of a candy bar. His brother ate some. They had 2/10 of the candy bar left. How much did his brother eat?

Way#1: Model with a tape diagram

Way#2: Solve with an equation, use a letter for the unknown

Explain your thinking:

Take From Change Unknown

4. Grandma Sandy made a delicious fruit punch. She made 2 liters of punch. Carl drank 580 ml. Kyle drank 556 ml. Sue drank 349 ml. Luke drank some also. There was 200 ml left. How much did Luke drink?

Way#1: Model with a tape diagram

Way#2: Solve with an equation, use a letter for the unknown

Explain your thinking:

TAKE FROM CHANGE UNKNOWN

5. The store had 4 meters of string for sale. Customer One bought 102.5 cm. Customer Two bought 126.7 cm. Customer Three bought some as well. The store had 1.5 meters left. How much did Customer Three buy?

Way#1: Model with an open number line

Way#2: Model with an equation, use a letter for the unknown

Explain your thinking:

TAKE FROM CHANGE UNKNOWN

6. In the morning 45,678 people downloaded Song A. In the afternoon, some more people downloaded Song A. By the evening, 100,000 people had downloaded the song. How many people downloaded the song in the afternoon?

Way#1: Model with a tape diagram

Way#2: Model with an equation, use a letter for the unknown

Explain your thinking:

TAKE FROM CHANGE UNKNOWN

7. David had $88.11. He spent $45.67 on clothes and $25.99 on shoes. He spent some more money on videos. He has $5.00 left. How much did he spend on videos?

Way#1: Model with a bar diagram

Way#2: Solve with numbers

Explain your thinking:

TAKE FROM CHANGE UNKNOWN

8. John made 1 liter of fruit punch. He drank 567 ml in the morning. Then he drank some more. He had 200 ml left. How much more did he drink?

Way#1: Model with a drawing

Way#2: Solve with an equation, use a letter for the unknown

Explain your thinking:

Chapter 2 Quiz: Take from Change Unknown Problems

Solve with a model:

1. Ted and his friends went to eat pizza. Ted ate 1/4 of the pizza. Tony at 2/8 of the pizza. Luke ate some of the pizza as well. There was 1/8 of the pizza left. How much did Luke eat?

2. Chong had $100. First, he spent $55.09 on clothes. Then he spent $24.09 on shoes and some more on videos. He had $10.00 left. How much did he spend on videos?

3. Mr. Cho left his house at 4:47. He came back at 8:29. How long was he gone?

4. Raul had 20 marbles. He gave 1/5 to his cousin, 2/10 to his brother and some to his sister. He had 7 left. How much did he give to his sister?

CHAPTER 3
TAKE FROM START UNKNOWN PROBLEMS

In these problems students are looking for how many things there were at the beginning of the story. In this type of story we only know that there was some amount and that there was a change (some things were taken away). We know what was taken away and how much was left. We are trying to find out how much we had in the beginning of the story.

PROBLEM	John had some marbles. He gave his brother 5. Now he has 10 left. How many did he have in the beginning?
MODEL	
EQUATION	? - 5 = 10 15 - 5 = 10

TAKE FROM START UNKNOWN

1. Mary went shopping. She spent $35.88 on books, $17.03 on jewelry and $45.98 on clothes. She had $10.00 left. How much did she have in the beginning?

Way#1: Model with a bar diagram

Way#2: Model with an equation, use a letter for the unknown

Explain your thinking:

TAKE FROM START UNKNOWN

2. Grandpa Pete drank some strawberry milk in the morning. In the afternoon, he drank 456 ml. Altogether he drank a liter of milk. How much did he drink in the morning?

Way#1: Solve with a drawing

Way#2: Solve with an equation, use a letter for the unknown

Explain your thinking:

Problem Solving with Math Models© 2012

Take From Start Unknown

3. Grandma Josie baked all morning. She used some flour for her cake, 391 grams of flour for her pies, and 354 grams of flour for her cookies. She used 1 kilogram of flour in total. How many grams of flour did she use for her cake?

Way#1: Solve with a tape diagram

Way#2: Solve with an equation, use a letter for the unknown

Explain your thinking:

TAKE FROM START UNKNOWN

4. Maribel left her house. She spent 2 1/2 hours at her friend's house. She spent 45 minutes at the mall. She spent 30 minutes at the swimming pool. She got home at 5:15. What time did she leave her house?

Way#1: Solve with a number line

Way#2: Solve with an illustration

Explain your thinking:

TAKE FROM START UNKNOWN

5. Some people downloaded Song B on Monday. On Tuesday, 35,678 more people downloaded Song B. On Wednesday, 17,894 more people downloaded Song B. In total, 70,000 people downloaded the song in 3 days. How many people downloaded the song on Monday?

Way#1: Model with a tape diagram

Way#2: Solve with numbers

Explain your thinking:

Take From Start Unknown

6. Jessica had some string. She used 24 inches to make a necklace, 18 inches to make a bracelet, and 3 inches to make a ring. She had 15 inches of string left. How much string did she have in the beginning? Did she use more than a yard of string to make her jewelry?

Way#1: Solve with a tape diagram

Way#2: Solve with numbers

Explain your thinking:

TAKE FROM START UNKNOWN

7. Dan used some flour in his huckleberry pies. He used 500g in his apple pie, 347g in his peach pie, 678 g in his blackberry pie. He had 256g left. How much did he have in the beginning?

Solve with a drawing

Explain your thinking:

TAKE FROM START UNKNOWN

8. Tracy ran in the morning. She ran 2/5 of a mile in the afternoon. In total, she ran 4/5 of mile. How far did she run in the morning?

Way#1: Solve with a number line

Way#2: Solve with numbers

Explain your thinking:

CHAPTER 3 QUIZ:
TAKE FROM START UNKNOWN PROBLEMS

Solve with a model:

1. On Monday, some people listened to Song A. On Tuesday, 3,456,908 more people listened to Song A. By Wednesday morning, 2,903,456 more people had listened to Song A. A total of 7,000,000 listened to Song A. How many people had listened to Song A on Monday?

2. Maria walked in the morning. In the afternoon, she walked 1/4 of a mile more. By the evening, she had walked 7/8 of a mile. How far did she walk in the morning?

3. Grandma Mabel made some pies. She had 2000 g of flour. She used some flour for the apple pie. She used 450 g for the peach pie and 398 g for the vanilla pie. There was 500 g left. How much did she use for the apple pie?

4. Mrs. Lou had some money. She spent some on jewelry. She then spent $55.67 on clothes, $45.88 on shoes and $12.77 on a purse. Altogether she spent $150. How much did she spend on jewelry?

UNIT 2 TEST:
TAKE FROM PROBLEMS

Solve with a model:

1. The bakery had 12 cookies. They sold ¼ in the morning and 1/3 in the afternoon. How many cookies did they sell in the morning? How many cookies did they sell in the afternoon?

2. Carol had $45.98. She spent $23.98 on jewelry. Then she spent some more on clothes. She had $10.00 left. How much money did she spend on clothes?

3.   Grandma made 2 liters of fruit punch. Luis drank 411 ml. Carl drank 589 ml. Sara drank 523ml. How many ml were left?

4.   Kelly arrived at the mall at 12:15. She left her house 45 minutes earlier. What time did she leave her house?

CHAPTER 1
PUT TOGETHER/TAKE APART PROBLEMS

These types of problems are about sets of things. In them we know both parts and we are looking for the whole. What distinguishes a Put Together/Take Apart Problem from an Add to Result Unknown problem is action. In a Put together/Take Apart Problem there is no action only a set of something.

PROBLEM	John had five red apples and five green ones. How many apples did he have altogether?
MODEL	
EQUATION	5 + 5 = 10

Put Together/Take Apart—Whole Unknown

1. Movie A grossed $29,456,399. Movie B grossed $15,987,999 at the box office. How much money did the 2 movies gross altogether?

Way#1: Model with a bar diagram

Way#2: Check your answer in a different way

Explain your thinking:

PUT TOGETHER/TAKE APART—WHOLE UNKNOWN

2. For Katie's birthday, her brother gave her $34.67, her sister gave her $35.99, and her parents gave her $90.88. How much money did she get for her birthday altogether?

Way#1: Solve with a drawing

Way#2: Solve with the formulas

Explain your thinking:

Put Together/Take Apart—Whole Unknown

3. Hong left his house at 8:30 am. He played soccer for 2 hours and 15 minutes. Then, he played basketball for 1 hour and 35 minutes. Then, he went swimming for 45 minutes. How long did he play sports? What time did he stop playing?

Solve with a number line diagram

Explain your thinking:

PUT TOGETHER/TAKE APART—WHOLE UNKNOWN

4. Todd biked 1/2 of a mile in the morning, ¾ of a mile in the afternoon, and 1/8 of a mile in the evening. How far did Todd bike altogether? Did he bike at least a mile?

Way#1: Solve with a number line

Way#2: Solve with an equation, use a letter for the unknown

Explain your thinking:

PUT TOGETHER/TAKE APART—WHOLE UNKNOWN

5. Grandma Daphne used 1/2 quart of chicken stock in her soup. She used 2 pints in her pie and 3 cups in her dressing. How many cups of chicken stock did Grandma use all total?

Way#1: Solve with a tape diagram

Way#2: Solve with an equation, use a letter for the unknown

Explain your thinking

PUT TOGETHER/TAKE APART—WHOLE UNKNOWN

6. Maria left her house at 5:10p.m. She spent 75 minutes at her aunt's house, 1 1/2 at her cousin's house, and 45 minutes at her grandmother's house. How long was she gone altogether in hours and minutes? What time did she get back home?

Solve with an open number line diagram

Explain your thinking:

Put Together/Take Apart - Whole Unknown

7. Grandpa Raul made a fruit punch for his grandkids. He used 1000 ml of pear juice, 450 ml of orange juice, 350 ml of grape juice, and 800 ml of apple juice. How many liters of fruit punch did he make?

Way#1: Solve with a tape diagram

Way#2: Solve with numbers

Explain your thinking:

PUT TOGETHER/TAKE APART—WHOLE UNKNOWN

8.   Macy wanted to exercise for 1 1/2 hours. She spent 34 minutes on the bike, 25 minutes on the treadmill, and 55 minutes swimming. Did she meet her goal? How many hours did she exercise?

Way#1: Solve with an open number line

Way#2: Solve with an equation, use a letter for the unknown

Explain your thinking:

> ## CHAPTER 1 QUIZ: PUT TOGETHER/ TAKE APART
> ## – WHOLE UNKNOWN PROBLEMS

Solve with a model:

1. Dana left her house at 12:37. She went to the mall for 1 hour and 20 minutes. She went to her cousin's house for 45 minutes. How long was she gone? What time did she get home?

2. This week, 3,456,789 people downloaded Song A. Song B was downloaded by 4,567,923 people. How many people downloaded both Song A and Song B?

Problem Solving with Math Models© 2012

3. Kate got some money for her birthday. Her grandma gave her $56.78. Her dad gave her $67.44. Her sister gave her $37.10. How much did she get for her birthday altogether?

4. Chef Lee used 456 ml of water in his soup. He used 259 ml in his punch. How much water did he use altogether?

CHAPTER 2
PUT TOGETHER/TAKE APART—PART UNKNOWN PROBLEMS

These types of problems are about sets of things. In them we know the total and one part of the set. We are looking for the other part of the set.

PROBLEM	John had ten apples. Five were red apples and the rest were green. How many apples were green?
MODEL	
EQUATION	$5 + ? = 10$ $\qquad$ $5 + 5 = 10$

PUT TOGETHER/TAKE APART - PART UNKNOWN

1. The bakery made 2 dozen cookies. Half of them were vanilla, 1/4 of them were chocolate and the rest were lemon. How many were lemon?

Way#1: Solve with a number line

Way#2: Solve with an equation, use a letter for the unknown

Explain your thinking:

PUT TOGETHER/TAKE APART - PART UNKNOWN

2. Lisa spent $250 total. She spent $129.99 on clothes, $78.67 on shoes and the rest on jewelry. How much did she spend on jewelry?

Way#1: Model with a tape diagram

Way#2: Solve with numbers

Explain your thinking:

PUT TOGETHER/TAKE APART - PART UNKNOWN

3.   Jake left his house at 10:20. He was gone for 4 and a half hours. He played sports for 2 1/2 hours. He then went to his friend's house for 45 minutes. He then went to the mall for the rest of the time. How long was he at the mall?

Way#1: Solve with numbers

Way#2: Check your answer a different way

Explain your thinking:

PUT TOGETHER/TAKE APART - PART UNKNOWN

4. The farm had 20 rabbits. One-fourth of them were black, one-fifth of them were white, and the rest were brown. What fraction of the rabbits were brown? How many were brown?

Way#1: Solve with a drawing

Way#2: Solve with an equation, use a letter for the unknown

Explain your thinking:

Put Together/Take Apart - Part Unknown

5. Mary used half of a kilogram of sugar to bake a pie. She used both brown and white sugar. She used 249 g of brown sugar and the rest was white sugar. How much white sugar did she use?

Solve with a number line

Explain your thinking:

PUT TOGETHER/TAKE APART - PART UNKNOWN

6. Grace ran 2 miles. She ran .6 miles in the morning, 1.2 miles in the afternoon and the rest in the evening. How many miles did she run in the evening?

Solve with a number line

Explain your thinking:

Put Together/Take Apart—Part Unknown

7.   Grandma Rose used 2 cups of milk to make pies and 2 cups to make soup. How many pints did she use altogether?

Way#1: Model with a drawing

Way#2: Solve with numbers

Explain your thinking:

PUT TOGETHER/TAKE APART - PART UNKNOWN

8. Derek had 20 marbles. Half of them were blue, 1/4 of them were orange and the rest were purple. How many were purple?

Way#1: Model with a tape diagram

Way#2: Solve with an equation, use a letter for the unknown

Explain your thinking:

CHAPTER 2 QUIZ:
PUT TOGETHER/TAKE APART – PART UNKNOWN

Solve with a model.

1. Doug had $250. He spent $85.67 on shoes, $99.77 on clothes, and the rest on video games. How much did he spend on video games?

2. The pizza store made 8 slices of pizza. Two-fourths of them were pepperoni, 2/8 of them were mushroom, and the rest were plain cheese. How many pieces were plain cheese?

3. John drank 1 liter of apple juice. He drank 257 ml in the morning, 356 ml in the afternoon, and the rest in the evening. How many ml did he drink in the evening?

4. Jackson cut 3 meters of wood. First, he cut 59 centimeters, then he cut another 128 centimeters, and then he cut some more. How many more centimeters of wood did he cut?

Problem Solving with Math Models© 2012

UNIT 3 TEST:
PUT TOGETHER/TAKE APART PROBLEMS

Solve with a model:

1. John had 40 marbles. One-fourth of them were green, one-fifth of them were blue, and the rest were orange. How many were orange?

2. Sandy biked 2.3 miles on Monday, 3.5 miles on Tuesday, 4.7 miles on Wednesday. On Thursday, she biked 0.9 miles. How many miles did she bike altogether?

3. Three thousand people went to the movies this weekend in our town. One thousand five-hundred thirty-three of them went to see action movies. The rest of them went to see comedies. How many people went to see comedies?

4. Maria made punch. She used 3 cups of pear juice, 2 pints of apple juice, a quart of orange juice and 1 cup of pineapple juice. How much punch did she make? How many pints did she make? How many quarts did she make?

CHAPTER 1
COMPARE DIFFERENCE UNKNOWN

In these problems students are comparing two or more amounts. They are comparing to find out what is the difference between the amounts. There are two versions of this type of story. One version uses the word more and one version uses the word fewer. The version with the word fewer is more difficult.

PROBLEM MORE VERSION	John had 12 marbles. Carl had 2 marbles. How many more marbles does John have than Carl?
MODEL	John Difference is 10 Carl 2 12
EQUATION	2 + ? = 12 2 + 10 = 12
PROBLEM FEWER VERSION	Carl had 2 marbles. John had 12 marbles. How many fewer marbles does Carl have than John?
MODEL	John Carl
EQUATION	12 − 2 =? 12 − 2 = 10

COMPARE FRACTIONS

1. Sonny ate 1/2 of a pizza. Ginny ate 1/5 of a pizza. Who ate more pizza?

Way#1: Solve with pictures

Way#2: Use the symbols <, >, or = to record the results of the comparison

Explain your thinking:

COMPARE FRACTIONS

2. Sarah has 0.58 of a dollar. Billy has 0.85 of a dollar. Who has more?

Way#1: Solve with a number line

Way#2: Use the symbols <, >, or = to record the results of the comparison

Explain your thinking:

COMPARE FRACTIONS

3. Jim and Brian ran in a race and finished at nearly the same time. Jim's time was 0.879 of a minute. Brian's time was 0.897 of a minute. Who finished the race first?

Way#1: Solve with an illustration or a number line

Way#2: Use the symbols <, >, or = to record the results of the comparison

Explain your thinking:

COMPARE FRACTION

4. Danny ate 5/6 of his personal pizza. Andy ate 2/3 of his. Who ate more?

Way#1: Solve with a picture

Way#2: Solve with a number line

Explain your thinking:

COMPARE MEASUREMENT

5. Amy cut two pieces of string. The first piece is 200 centimeters long. The second piece is 1 meter long. Which piece of string is longer?

Solve with an illustration

Explain your thinking:

COMPARE VOLUME

6. There are two boxes on the table. The first box has a length of 4 inches, a width of 5 inches, and a height of 3 inches. The second box has a length of 2 inches, a width of 6 inches, and a height of 6 inches. Which box has the larger volume?

Solve with a formula

Explain your thinking:

COMPARE VOLUME

7. Denise is building an aquarium. She wants to purchase a large fish tank. Fish Tank A has a length of 8 feet, a width of 3 feet, and a height of 5 feet. Fish Tank B has a length of 7 feet, a width of 6 feet, and a height of 4 feet. Which fish tank has the larger volume?

Solve with a formula

Explain your thinking:

COMPARE USING A LINE PLOT

8. Maggie and her dad went fishing. They caught several fish with the following lengths in feet:

   1/4, 1/4, 2/4, 2/4, 2/4, 3/4, 3/4, 4/4, 4/4, 4/4

Make a line plot for the data

What is the total length of all the fish that were 2/4 of a foot long?

What is the difference between the longest and shortest fish?

CHAPTER 1 QUIZ:
COMPARE PROBLEMS

Solve with a model:

1. Brendan cut two lengths of string. The first piece was 0.256 cm long. The second was 0.387 cm long. Which piece of string was longer?

2. Ginger ate 7/8 of her candy bar. Sal ate 5/6 of his. Who ate more?

3. Chris and Wendy are making fruit punch. The punch calls for two quarts of apple juice and 6 cups of grape juice. Which juice do they need more of?

4. Marty has two boxes. One box is 5 inches long, 8 inches wide, and 3 inches high. The second box is 6 inches long, 5 inches wide, and 3 inches high. Which box has the larger volume?

5. Brian and Jamie are measuring crickets in science class. The lengths of the crickets (in inches) are:

    2/6, 3/6, 3/6, 3/6, 4/6, 6/6, 6/6

    Create a line plot for the data

What is the difference between the length of the shortest and longest crickets?

CHAPTER 2
COMPARISON – BIGGER PART UNKNOWN

In these problems students are comparing two or more amounts. They are comparing to find out who had the bigger part. There are two versions of this type of story. One version uses the word more and one version uses the word fewer. The version with the word fewer is more difficult.

PROBLEM MORE VERSION	John has 5 more marbles than Carl. Carl has 2 marbles. How many marbles does John have?
MODEL	7 total John Carl
EQUATION	$5 + 2 = ?$ $5 + 2 = 7$

PROBLEM FEWER VERSION	Carl has 3 fewer marbles than John? Carl has 2 marbles. How many marbles does John have?
MODEL	Carl John 5 total
	$2 + 3 = ?$ $2 + 3 = 5$

COMPARISON – BIGGER PART UNKNOWN

1. Tim has 4/10 of a dollar. Mike has 2/10 more than he does. How much money does Mike have?

Way#1: Solve with a number line

Way#2: Solve with numbers

Explain your thinking:

COMPARISON – BIGGER PART UNKNOWN

2. Harrison is weighing his two kittens. The first kitten weighs 0.56 pounds. The second kitten weighs 0.24 pounds more. How much does the second kitten weigh?

Way#1: Model with a number line

Way#2: Solve with numbers

Explain your thinking:

COMPARISON – BIGGER PART UNKNOWN

3. Andy used 0.464 grams of flour to make a pizza. He used .256 more grams to make a small pie. How much flour did he use to make the pie?

Way#1: Solve with a number line

Way#2: Solve with numbers

Explain your thinking:

COMPARISON – BIGGER PART UNKNOWN

4. Steve ate 2/8 of a pizza. His brother ate ¼ more than he did. How much pizza did his brother eat?

Way#1: Solve with an illustration

Way#2: Solve with number line

Explain your thinking:

COMPARISON – BIGGER PART UNKNOWN

5. Mike drank 2 pints of milk. Chris drank a quart more than he did. How many pints of milk did Chris drink?

Solve with an illustration

Explain your thinking:

Problem Solving with Math Models© 2012

COMPARISON – BIGGER PART UNKNOWN

6. Doug has 50 nickels and 4 dimes. Jonathan has 25 cents more than he does. How much does Jonathan have?

Solve with numbers

Explain your thinking:

COMPARISON – BIGGER PART UNKNOWN

7. Ginger walked 2/5 of a mile in the morning. In the afternoon she walked 2/10 of a mile farther. How far did she walk in the afternoon?

Solve using a formula

Explain your thinking:

Problem Solving with Math Models© 2012

COMPARISON – BIGGER PART UNKNOWN

8. Dana used 1 1/2 cups of sugar to make a cake. She used 1/4 more of a cup of sugar for the frosting. How much sugar did she use in the frosting?

Way#1: Solve with an illustration

Way#2: Solve with a number line

Explain your thinking:

CHAPTER 2 QUIZ:
COMPARE BIGGER PART UNKNOWN

Solve with a model:

1. Bag A weighed 5 kilos. Bag B weighed 2000 g more. How much did Bag B weigh?

2. Dylan used 2/6 of a pumpkin to make pumpkin pie. He used 1/3 more than that to make pumpkin bread. How much of the pumpkin did he use to make pumpkin bread?

3. Kathleen drank 2 pints of orange juice. Bill drank 2 more cups of juice than she did. How many pints did he drink?

4. Jamal ran 5/10 of a mile in the morning. In the afternoon he ran 1/2 a further than he ran in the morning. How far did he run in the afternoon?

CHAPTER 3
COMPARISON – SMALLER PART UNKNOWN

In these problems students are comparing two or more amounts. They are comparing to find out who has the smaller amount. There are two versions of this type of story. One version uses the word more and one version uses the word fewer. The version with the word fewer is more difficult.

PROBLEM MORE VERSION	John had 4 more marbles than Carl. John had 5 marbles. How many marbles did Carl have?
MODEL	John Carl
EQUATION	5 – 4 = ? 5 – 4 = 1

PROBLEM FEWER VERSION	Carl had 10 fewer marbles than John. John had 12 marbles. How many marbles did Carl have?
MODEL	John Carl
EQUATION	12 – 10 = ? 12 – 10 = 2

COMPARISON – SMALLER PART UNKNOWN

1. Kate ran 1/2 a mile in the morning. In the afternoon, she ran 1/4 of a mile less than she did in the morning. How far did Kate run in the afternoon?

Way#1: Solve with a number line

Way#2: Solve with numbers

Explain your thinking:

COMPARISON – SMALLER PART UNKNOWN

2. Bob had $0.53 of a dollar in his pocket. He had $0.27 of a dollar less in his wallet. How much of a dollar did he have in his wallet?

Way#1: Model with a number line

Way#2: Solve with numbers

Explain your thinking:

COMPARISON – SMALLER PART UNKNOWN

3.   It took 0.736 minutes to download Song A. It took 0.249 fewer minutes to download Song B. How long did it take to download Song B?

Way#1: Solve with numbers

Way#2: Check a different way

Explain your thinking:

COMPARISON – SMALLER PART UNKNOWN

4. Jerry ate 5/6 of a cake. Tim ate 2/3 less of a cake the same size. How much cake did Tim eat?

Way#1: Solve with drawing

Way#2: Solve with numbers

Explain your thinking:

COMPARISON – SMALLER PART UNKNOWN

5. Sandy bought 2 meters of purple string. She bought 100 cm less of pink string. How many meters of pink string did she buy?

Way#1: Model with a drawing

Way#2: Show with numbers

Explain your thinking:

COMPARISON – SMALLER PART UNKNOWN

6. Clark ran 7/8 of a mile in the morning. In the afternoon he ran 1/2 mile less than he ran in the morning. How far did he run in the afternoon?

Solve using a formula

Explain your thinking:

COMPARISON – SMALLER PART UNKNOWN

7. Lucy went to the mall for 180 minutes. Carol went to the mall for 1 hour less than Lucy. How long was Carol at the mall?

Way#1: Model with a number line

Way#2: Solve with numbers

Explain your thinking:

COMPARISON – SMALLER PART UNKNOWN

8. Danny used a gallon of grape juice in his grape punch. He used 4 pints less in his regular fruit punch. How many quarts did he use in his regular fruit punch?

Solve with diagram

Explain your thinking:

CHAPTER 3 QUIZ:
COMPARE SMALLER UNKNOWN PROBLEMS

Solve with a model:

1. Billy has $23.45. Kim has $3.54 less money. How much money does Kim have?

2. Bill uses 3/4 of a cup of sugar in his cake. He uses 1/2 a cup less in his brownies. How much sugar does he use in his brownies?

3. Sarah ran 5 kilometers on Monday. She ran half that distance on Tuesday. How many meters did she run on Tuesday?

4. Clark used 2/3 a cup of flour for his cookies. He used 1/2 of a cup more for his brownies. How much flour did he use for his brownies?

UNIT 4 TEST:
COMPARE PROBLEMS

Solve with a model:

1. Weng made 0.465 kilograms of fudge. Adam made 0.549 more kilograms of fudge. How many kilograms of fudge did Adam make? How much fudge they make altogether?

2. Jenny ran 3/4 of a mile. Cynthia ran 7/8 of a mile. Who ran farther? How much farther?

3. Marta and Melissa bought sub sandwiches that were the same size. Marta ate 5/6 of hers. Melissa ate 1/3 less of hers. How much of her sub did she eat?

4. Tim is purchasing two fish tanks, one for his fish and one for his turtles. The fish tank for his fish is 4 feet long, 3 feet wide, and 2 feet deep. The fish tank for his turtles is 5 feet long, 4 feet wide, and 3 feet deep. Which fish tank is larger? How much larger?

NAME:

DATE:

Solve the problems. Show your work by drawing a picture, using a number line, making a table, or using formulas.

1. Paul had $154.88. His father gave him $77.45. How much money does Paul have now?

2. Grandpa Andre was making pies. He used 545 grams of sugar total. He used 360 grams in his apple pie and the rest in his peach pie. How much sugar did he use in his peach pie?

3. Jenny ran in the morning and then ran some more in the evening. In the evening she ran 2.5 miles. Altogether, she ran 5.3 miles. How far did she run in the morning?

4. Ben drank 636 ml of milk. Sarah drank 845 ml of milk. How much more milk did Sarah drink than Ben?

5. Keith has $378. He bought some shoes for $103, three ties for $78, a watch for $56, and a pair of pants. He has $53 left. How much was the pair of pants?

6. On Monday, Song A had 456,789 downloads. The song had more downloads on Tuesday. By Wednesday there were 700,000 downloads. How many downloads were there on Tuesday?

7. Olivia drank 1/2 a quart of apple juice in the morning. She drank a pint of apple juice at lunch and 2 cups of apple juice at dinner. How much apple juice, in cups, did she drink during the day?

8. Grandma made 3 liters of punch. In the morning her grandchildren drank 1500 ml. In the afternoon they drank another liter. How many ml of punch was left?

9. Rose and Jan were reading the same book for school. Rose read 5/6 of the book. Jan read 3/4 of the book. Who read more?

10. Danny has 3,783 mm of string. Billy has 2 meters of string. Who has more string?

11. Jamie is purchasing a fish tank for her turtles. She has two turtles and wants the largest tank she can find for them. Tank A is 5 feet long, 4 feet wide, and 2 feet deep. Tank B is 4 feet long, 4 feet wide, and 3 feet deep. What is the volume of each tank? Which tank will Jamie buy?

12. Brian and Jamie are baking cakes. In total, they use 1 kilogram of flour. They use 326 grams in their chocolate cake and the rest in a two layer cake. How much flour did they use in the two layer cake?

13. Sandy's science class is measuring crickets. The measurements are (in inches):

    1/8, 1/8, 1/4, 1/4, 1/4, 1/4, 1/4, 1/2, 3/4, 1

    Create a line plot to display the data.

What is the difference between the longest and shortest crickets?

What is the combined measurement of all the crickets that are 1/2 an inch or bigger?

14. Laila brags that she drank a gallon of water yesterday. Nathan drank one quart less. How many pints of water did Nathan drink yesterday?

15. JoJo left her house early this morning. She went to the gym for an hour and a half. She visited her mother for 45 minutes. Then she dropped a letter off at the post office, which took ten minutes. The drive home took 15 minutes. She arrived home by 11:15. What time did she leave her house that morning?

Unit 1—Add to Problems

Chapter 1: Add to Result Unknown Problems

1. 6 pints
2. $362.87
3. 1 ¼ cups
4. 2,221 ml
5. 289,653 views
6. 21/4 OR 5 ¼ inches
7. 325.48 miles
8. Yes; 8 meters

Chapter 1 Quiz: Add to Result Unknown

1. 6.04 miles
2. 4,657ml
3. 9/8 OR 1 1/8 cups
4. 5 yards, 1.5 feet

Chapter 2: Add to Change Unknown Problems

1. 1,541 grams OR 1 kilogram, 541 grams
2. 39 minutes
3. ¾ of a cup
4. 813 ml
5. $16.81
6. $0.75
7. 3,100 ml OR 3 liters, 100 ml
8. 2 ¼ pounds

Chapter 2 Quiz: Add to Change Unknown Problem

1. 4 hours, 42 minutes
2. 1.5 liters
3. 1.6 OR 1 6/10 OR 1 3/5 miles
4. $17.79

Chapter 3: Add to Start Unknown

1. 8.093 downloads
2. 11:30
3. $15.50
4. 74.22 miles
5. 5.5 liters
6. 2,513 grams
7. 1 quart
8. 1 ½ miles

Chapter 3 Quiz: Add to Start Unknown Problems

1. $23.45
2. 2:10
3. 644 ml
4. 64,211 hits

UNIT 1 TEST: ADDITION PROBLEMS

1. 63 cm
2. 11/12 of a cup
3. 2 quarts and 3 cups
4. $24.55

Unit 2—Take From Problems

Chapter 1: Take From Result Unknown

1. $50.01
2. 1,279 ml
3. 7 shelves
4. 2 pints
5. 125 minutes; 25 minutes
6. 10 cupcakes; 2 cupcakes
7. 8/10 OR 4/5; 2/10 OR 1/5

Chapter 1 Quiz: Take From Result Unknown Problems

1. $23.35
2. 1,500 grams or 1.5 kilograms
3. 1 meter, 67 centimeters OR 167 cm
4. 3 brownies

Chapter 2: Take From Change Unknown Problems

1. 2 pints
2. 2 hours, 50 minutes
3. 3/5 of the candy bar
4. 315 ml
5. 20.8 cm
6. 54,322 people
7. $11.45
8. 233 ml

Chapter 2 Quiz: Take From Change Unknown Problems

1. 3/8 of the pizza
2. $10.82
3. 3 hours, 42 minutes
4. 5 marbles

Chapter 3: Take From Start Unknown Problems

1. $108.89
2. 544 ml
3. 255 grams
4. 1:30
5. 16,428 people
6. 60 inches; yes
7. 1,781 g
8. 2/5 of a mile

Chapter 3 Quiz: Take From Start Unknown Problems

1. 639,636 people
2. 5/8 of a mile
3. 652 grams
4. $35.68

UNIT 2 TEST: TAKE FROM PROBLMES

1. 3 cookies; 4 cookies
2. $12
3. 477 ml
4. 11:30

Unit 3—Put Together/Take Apart Problems

Chapter 1: Put Together/Take Apart— Whole Unknown Problems

1. $45,444,398
2. $161.54
3. 4 hours, 35 minutes; 1:05
4. 11/8 OR 1 3/8; yes
5. 9 cups
6. 3 hours, 30 minutes; 8:40
7. 2.6 liters OR 2 liters, 600 ml
8. Yes; 1 hour, 54 minutes

Chapter 1 Quiz: Put Together/Take Apart—Whole Unknown Problems

1. 2 hours, 5 minutes; 2:42
2. 8,024,712 people
3. $161.32
4. 715 ml

Chapter 2: Put Together/Take Apart—Part Unknown Problems

1. 6 lemon cookies
2. $41.34
3. 45 minutes
4. 11/20; 11 were brown
5. 251 grams
6. 0.2 miles
7. 2 pints
8. 5 purple

Chapter 2 Quiz: Put Together/Take Apart—Part Unknown Problems

1. $64.56
2. 2 slices
3. 387 ml
4. 113 cm

UNIT 3 TEST: PUT TOGETHER/TAKE APART PROBLEMS

1. 22 orange marbles
2. 10.59
3. 1,467 people
4. 12 cups; 3 quarts

Unit 4—Comparison—Difference Unknown Problems

Chapter 1: Compare Fraction Problems

1. Sonny; 0.6 > 0.4
2. Billy; 0.58 < 0.85
3. Jim; 0.879 < 0.897
4. Danny
5. 200 centimeters
6. The second box
7. Fish Tank B
8. 6/4 OR 1 2/4 OR 1 ½ ; ¾ of a foot

Chapter 1 Quiz: Compare Problems

1. The second piece
2. Ginger
3. Apple juice
4. The first box
5. 4/6 OR 2/3

Chapter 2: Comparison—Bigger Part Unknown Problems

1. 0.6 of a dollar OR $0.60
2. 0.8 pounds
3. 0.72 grams
4. ½ of the pizza
5. 4 pints
6. $3.15
7. 3/5
8. 1 3/4

Chapter 2 Quiz: Comparison—Bigger Part Unknown Problems

1. 5.2 km
2. 2/3 of the pumpkin
3. 3 pints
4. 1 mile

Chapter 3: Comparison—Smaller Part Unknown Problems

1. ¼ of a mile
2. 0.26 of a dollar OR $0.26
3. 0.487
4. 1/6 of his cake
5. 1 meter
6. 3/8 of a mile
7. 2 hours
8. 2 quarts

Chapter 3 Quiz: Comparison Smaller Unknown Problems

1. $19.91
2. ¼ of a cup
3. 2.5
4. 1 1/6 cups

UNIT 4 TEST: COMPARE PROBLEMS

1. 1.014 kg; 0.084 kg
2. Cynthia; 1/8 of a mile
3. 1/2
4. The turtle tank; 36 cubic feet larger

FINAL WORD PROBLEM TEST— FIFTH GRADE

1. $232.33
2. 185 grams
3. 2.8 miles
4. 209 ml
5. $88
6. 243,2111 downloads
7. 6 cups
8. 500
9. Rose
10. Danny
11. 40 cubic feet; 48 cubic feet; Tank B
12. 674 grams
13. 7/8 of an inch; 2 ¾ inches
14. 6 pints
15. 8:35

REFERENCES

Carpenter, T., Fennema, E., Franke, M., Levi, L., & Empson, S. (1999). *Children's Mathematics: Cognitively Guided Instruction*. Portsmouth, NH: Heinemann.

Common Core Standards Writing Team (Bill McCullum, lead author). (2012, June 23). *Progressions for the common core state standards in mathematics: Geometry (draft)*. Retrieved from: www.commoncoretools.wordpress.com.

Common Core Standards Writing Team (Bill McCullum, lead author). (2012, June 23). *Progressions for the common core state standards in mathematics: Geometric measurement (draft)*. Retrieved from: www.commoncoretools.wordpress.com.

Common Core Standards Writing Team (Bill McCullum, lead author). (2011, June 20). *Progressions for the common core state standards in mathematics: K-3, Categorical data; Grades 2-5, Measurement Data (draft)*. Retrieved from: www.commoncoretools.wordpress.com.

Common Core Standards Writing Team (Bill McCullum, lead author). (2011, May 29). *Progressions for the common core state standards in mathematics: K, Counting and cardinality; K-5, operations and algebraic thinking (draft)*. Retrieved from: www.commoncoretools.wordpress.com.

Common Core Standards Writing Team (Bill McCullum, lead author). (2011, April 7). *Progressions for the common core state standards in mathematics: K-5, Number and operations in base ten (draft)*. Retrieved from: www.commoncoretools.wordpress.com.

Common Core Standards Writing Team (Bill McCullum, lead author). (2011, July 12). *Progressions for the common core state standards in mathematics: 3-5 Number and operations - fractions (draft)*. Retrieved from: www.commoncoretools.wordpress.com.

Peterson, P. L., Carpenter, T. P., & Loef, M. (1989). *Teachers' Pedagogical Content Beliefs in Mathematics. Cognition and Instruction*, Vol. 6, No. 1, pp. 1-40.

Made in the USA
Lexington, KY
11 October 2014